HELPING CHILDREN COPE WITH DIVORCE

A Practical Resource Guide for *Mom and Dad Break Up*

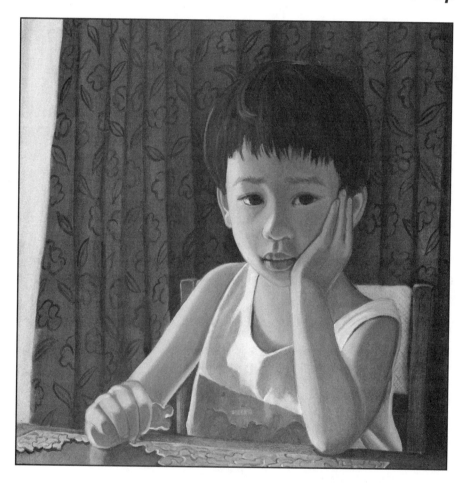

By Joan Singleton Prestine

Fearon Teacher Aids
A Division of Frank Schaffer Publications, Inc.

Executive Editor: Jeri Cipriano
Cover and Inside Illustration: Virginia Kylberg

This Fearon Teacher Aids product was formerly manufactured and distributed by American Teaching Aids, Inc., a subsidiary of Silver Burdett Ginn, and is now manufactured and distributed by Frank Schaffer Publications, Inc. FEARON, FEARON TEACHER AIDS, and the FEARON balloon logo are marks used under license from Simon & Schuster, Inc.

© **Fearon Teacher Aids**
A Division of Frank Schaffer Publications, Inc.
23740 Hawthorne Boulevard
Torrance, CA 90505-5927

© 1996 Fearon Teacher Aids. All rights reserved. Printed in the United States of America. This publication, or parts thereof, may not be reproduced in any form by photographic, electronic, mechanical, or any other method, for any use, including information storage and retrieval, without written permission from the publisher. Student reproducibles excepted.

ISBN 0-86653-858-5

5 6 7 8 9 MAL 01 00

Acknowledgments

I want to thank the following people for their support, encouragement, and expertise. Their suggestions were invaluable.

Doug Prestine, my husband, best friend and
  computer expert

Virginia Kylberg, gifted artist

Sandy Hatch and Ann Alper, marriage, family, and
  child counselors

Joann Burch, Jeri Ferris, Debbie Kachidurian, and
  Davida Kristy, teachers

Nadine Davidson and Celeste Mannis, fellow authors

Elaine Bradish, wise friend and consultant

The Prestine and Singleton families, loyal supporters

Contents

Preface

There are three guarantees in life: birth, death, and change. The varied composition of families today exemplify change. The traditional definition of a family has evolved in the last twenty years beyond the Father, Mother, and children model. This model is now just one of many accepted family structures. Families today may include one parent and a child or children; grandparents and grandchildren; or father, stepmother, and children. Whatever the structure of a family, it still:

- provides food, clothing, and shelter

- provides love

- teaches values and customs

Helping Children Cope With Divorce was written to help adults assist young children in finding positive responses to the feelings that result from the separation and divorce of their parents. It is my hope that children will understand that regardless of the structure of their family, their family is a *family*. I want children to discuss openly their hopes and dreams as well as their sadness and anger as they accept changes that take place in their lives.

About *Mom and Dad Break Up*

The *Mom and Dad Break Up* picturebook is designed to help children understand the feelings and responses they may have when their parents divorce or separate. Read the book and discuss the story with children as a prelude to using the activities outlined in this resource.

In the story, the boy discovers that sometimes things that seem to belong together, like Mom and Dad, don't always stay together. The boy feels angry and doesn't want to play with his friends. Alone, he goes into his room and pounds the pillow. He is overcome with sadness, and rather than skate with his friend Anthony, the boy cries. Later in the story, the boy dreams that he and his mom and dad are together again and happy. Even though the boy knows it's not his fault that his parents are divorcing, he still plans surprise parties to get them back together. When the surprise parties don't work, he doesn't give up hope. He then pretends to be sick and to need both of his parents to make him better, but his parents stay divorced.

Finally, the boy realizes that he is not going to live with both Mom and Dad. He accepts that he still has both parents—albeit separately—and that each parent can still have fun with him, and that, most importantly, Mom and Dad love him.

Introduction

Today, children of divorce are accepted by their peers, and are not viewed as outcasts. In fact, most children of divorce don't have a problem telling their friends that their parents are divorced. Nevertheless, divorce or separation is a traumatic event in children's lives, according to Marianne Neifert, M.D., in her book *Dr. Mom's Parenting Guide.* After all, their entire world has been turned upside down through no fault of their own.

After divorce, children often feel that they have no control over what is happening in their lives. They experience a variety of unsettling feelings because they love both parents equally, but often find themselves living with one parent and seeing the non-custodial parent less frequently. There can be other changes created by a divorce, including: a mother who may have to go to work; a drop in the family's standard of living; moving to a new home; or being separated from a sibling. Probably neither parent has as much time or energy for the children as before.

As adults, we need to remember to listen to the feelings and thoughts of children. With the divorce rate in the United States approaching 50%, nearly all children will experience the direct or indirect effects of divorce through their relatives or friends. Despite the prevalence of divorce, each child experiences it individually, and many children do not openly discuss the details. Adults can learn how to help children deal with their emotions in positive ways. Children can also be taught that they can choose to respond negatively or positively to their feelings.

Helping Children Cope with Divorce is a guide to help teachers, parents, and other adults assist children in understanding and dealing with the emotions that arise from the experience of divorce. This resource provides practical suggestions and activities for communicating with children, recognizing their feelings, and helping them cope constructively with the changes that come with divorce as presented in the picturebook *Mom and Dad Break Up.*

Talking It Over

Children mainly learn about their parents' problems through observation. When their parents aren't getting along, children are likely to see arguing, extended silences, or even fighting. Some parents think they are protecting their children by not telling them what is going on. Other parents feel it is none of their children's business or that their children are too young to understand.

It is better to discuss some of the details with children, as they are usually aware that there's a problem. For children experiencing divorce, talking about what they have seen and heard, what they think and feel, and what they presently see happening is part of the healing process. Each child will cope differently with the trauma of a divorce. The following activities may help children discuss divorce and their feelings about it in a comfortable way.

Just Talking

Adults can become so immersed in their own lives that they forget to spend time talking with children. Sitting on the floor or getting to eye level with children establishes a relaxing posture that often leads to informal discussion. Talking one-to-one for a few minutes each day can make children feel more secure. Discuss school, friends, and hobbies. The conversation may then move to family issues. Talking in such an informal manner helps children open up at a time when they may feel that their world is closing in on them.

In Charge

Sometimes it is easier for children to talk about difficult topics, like divorce, when they feel they have some control over the conversation. Let them choose when and where they want to talk. You may suggest sitting on the floor, lying under a tree, or going for a walk. Giving children a little control helps them realize that they are in charge of something in their lives.

Thinking It Through

Some children enjoy problem-solving activities such as puzzles. Working on a puzzle is quieting for these children. As they put puzzle pieces in place, take the opportunity to encourage them to think out loud about what is going on with their families.

So Caring

It is comforting for some children to take care of others. Sometimes it is easier for them to talk about how they think their Mom, Dad, brother, or sister feels rather than talking about their own feelings. Observe how children talk to and care for others; it can provide clues as to how they want to be cared for.

Nix Yes and No

Children often feel more comfortable with "yes" and "no" responses to questions. Ask open-ended questions to give children an opportunity to answer questions in sentences, not just with a *yes or a no*. A parent might ask open-ended questions such as these: *Tell me what you think about [Mom/Dad] and me not getting along. . . I'd like to hear about. . . Tell me how you feel when. . .* Remember that questions beginning with *what, when*, and *where* can help you better understand how the child is handling the divorce.

Responding to Divorce

It is common for children who experience divorce to feel a burst of miserable feelings. Knowing how to respond to these feelings helps children adjust to the divorce more easily. Help children understand that for every action there is a feeling about an action. By teaching children that their responses have natural consequences, children begin to learn to choose ways to deal with these emotions. And when children have a feeling, they respond to it in some way. Actions evoke feelings and those feelings bring about responses. This cycle—action, feeling, response—is universal.

It is helpful for children to know that their miserable feelings are normal. The following list shows some typical feelings and responses children involved in a divorce may go through.

Feeling	Response
shock or denial	won't accept divorce
discouraged	gives up in school
angry	yells, hits, kicks
sad	cries
lonely	withdraws from friends
hopeless	plots to fix parents
guilty	blames self for divorce
helpless	cleans whole house
sick	develops stomachache
scared	fears abandonment
better	accepts and adjusts

The ages of the children involved in a divorce can affect how they react to the divorce, according to Dr. Neil Kalter in his book *Growing Up with Divorce*. The following list, organized developmentally, indicates typical responses of children involved in divorce and how adults might respond.

- Infants and toddlers may have trouble being separated from their primary caregiver. To form a relationship with the absent parent, children need shorter, but more frequent visits.

- Preschoolers and children under eight years old tend to blame themselves for the divorce. They also fear that both parents may abandon them. Keeping a schedule reassures children that their parents are there for them.

- Older elementary-school-age children may feel both love and anger toward their parents. Some children are openly hostile when what they really want is to be loved or hugged. Children this age need words of comfort and to spend time with parents on shared activities.

- Teen-agers may keep their feelings to themselves or turn their feelings into negative actions such as drug taking or skipping school. A firm structure and open communication helps to maintain continuity in their lives.

In addition to the age factor, children within the same family may exhibit different feelings and behaviors in response to the divorce. Some children regress and temporarily act less mature. Because children's emotions are at a peak, it is important to remember that they may seem happy and well-adjusted one day and angry or sad the next. What works with a child one day may not work the next day, week, or month. Children's feelings and behavior may go up and down like a roller coaster, requiring different adult strategies.

Listen, Listen, Listen

Children learn to listen to you, if you listen to them. Let them know that you care by saying, "I'm going to be a good listener. I want to hear everything you have to say." After the child finishes talking, remember to clarify or summarize what the child has said.

Tell Me Why

Young children have many questions: *Why do you argue? Why can't you be nice to each other? Why aren't we like other families? Why don't you stay married? Do you love me?* Answer their questions simply and briefly. Children aren't looking for long-winded answers, but they want and need responses.

Building Self-Esteem

It is common for parents to experience low self-esteem after a divorce, according to Marianne Neifert, M.D. Children do, too. As parents become critical of themselves, some children can become critical of themselves as well. Occasionally, children wish to be the opposite of who they are: for example, an aggressive child may long to be gentle. The following activities are designed to help children accept themselves and rebuild self-esteem.

The Best Me
Encourage children to list the things that they like about themselves. For example: *I am smart, I stand tall, I look people in the eye, I am a good artist, I run fast, I read every day, I do my homework, I smile, I am lovable, I am funny, I am nice.* Let them know that they can always add to the list. Then help them find a light-colored T-shirt. Insert a piece of cardboard inside the T-shirt. With permanent markers have children select key words from their lists and write or dictate the words they want on their T-shirts. Urge them to wear their T-shirts often.

Say It Once
Maxims, proverbs, and sayings can be comforting for some children. Help children cut construction paper into strips. Then help children write their own sayings or copy maxims, proverbs, or sayings that make them feel good. Sometimes the maxims, proverbs, and sayings children hear over and over are the most comforting. For example:

> *Sticks and stones may break my bones, but names will never hurt me.*
> *I think I can, I think I can, I think I can. . .*
>   *I thought I could!*
> *One day at a time.*

Invite children to decorate their posters. When they are finished, help them to glue magnets to the backs of their sayings. Encourage children to post the maxims, proverbs, and sayings in different places in their homes.

Picture This!

Many times children are more comfortable expressing themselves artistically rather than verbally. Select a bulletin board for them to decorate with pictures from old magazines. Encourage children to talk about the items they place on the bulletin board. Talk with them about how special they are. Help them decorate the bulletin board. Then stand back and view it with pride.

Using Activities

Activities are excellent ways to encourage children to express their feelings. The practical activities in this resource guide help children understand their feelings. The activities can reassure children that it is normal to have strong feelings and responses to a divorce. In addition, the activities provide children with specific tasks that help them work through their feelings. The activities in this resource are not intended to address the needs of children who have severe emotional or adjustment problems related to a divorce. These children may need to receive special professional guidance.

Suggestions for Implementing the Activities

- Don't tell children how to feel or respond. Give basic directions, but allow children the freedom to create their own projects. Their projects will be more meaningful to them if children can create according to their own visions in a loosely structured environment.

- Provide a play environment in which activities can be introduced. This type of environment encourages children to approach feelings and thoughts that might otherwise be too uncomfortable to deal with.

- Some children choose to engage in one activity over and over, and not to participate in others. That's all right. An activity may be perfect for one child and not for another. Feel free to rotate activities to accommodate the needs of children in your care.

- The thoughts and feelings children experience while participating in a project are important considerations. Feelings that children once held for their family before the divorce may be re-experienced. Tears may flow. Comment on children's sad feelings and then help them put their feelings into words.

- It may be difficult for you to accurately assess how a child dealing with divorce is doing. If you have questions about the adjustment some children are making, save examples of their work. Include a date on the back of each activity so a chronological progression is easy to follow. You might also keep notes or comments on verbal responses to share with a child's school or therapist.

The activities that follow are divided into sections that relate to some of the feelings children may experience as conveyed in the picture *Mom and Dad Break Up*. After listening to the children's comments and questions and helping them express how they feel, choose activities that are appropriate for each child's particular emotional needs.

Feeling Shock

"That's not the way it's supposed to be."

These words from the picturebook *Mom and Dad Break Up* convey the feelings children often have when they experience the shock and denial that can accompany the divorce of their parents.

Children feel the effects of divorce as soon as they hear about it. It doesn't matter how old the child is—shock and denial usually set in. As painful or strained as family life may have been, it's what the child knows. Children's lives revolve around their families; family is the most important thing to them.

Denial is often a "safe haven" for children who aren't ready to acknowledge their parents' problems. Shock and denial allow children to feel that there's always a chance the problem will go away. The following activities may help children understand that their parents are getting divorced and are not getting back together.

I'll Never Tell

Some children are unable to accept divorce, so they don't discuss it with friends. They may, however, express feelings to their pets and stuffed toys. These friends are safe and give unconditional love. Encourage children to share as much as possible with their pets or toys. After sharing with pets and toys, children may be more open to sharing their thoughts with others.

Practice Makes Perfect

Occasionally, children have a hard time answering questions about divorce. They want to think their family is still okay, so they make up answers. Often, making up answers is less painful than answering honestly. It is comforting for children to have ready-made answers for questions that are bound to come up. Role-play with children so they can practice what they want to say when people ask questions.

Family Tree

On a large piece of paper, draw a tree with many branches. Explain to children the concept of a family tree. Help them understand that their family includes *generations* of people—grandparents, aunts, uncles, cousins, and so on. Have children write the names of everyone they know in their immediate and extended family on colorful paper leaves. Have them glue the names onto their trees. Suggest that children count how many people are in their family. Sometimes it is helpful for children to see that their family is larger than their immediate family. Encourage them to seek out other family members for support in dealing with the divorce.

Puzzler

Figuring out what is going on with a family during a divorce can be tough, especially for children. Glue a family photograph or picture on to a piece of cardboard. Then cut the picture into large pieces. While the child is putting the pieces of the puzzle back together, encourage conversation about what is going on and how the child feels about his or her family. Help the child understand that what is happening is not his or her fault; that though the child has no control over what the parents choose, Mom and Dad will always be Mom and Dad.

Feeling Discouraged

**"Sometimes things that belong together,
like Mom and Dad, break up.
And sometimes no one,
not even me, can fix them."**

These words from the picturebook *Mom and Dad Break
Up* convey the feeling of discouragement that children have
following the divorce of their parents.

Regardless of how old the children are, divorce usually
means feelings of loss. Divorce may be as traumatic for
some children as death. They see divorce as the death of
their family. The closeness children feel with their parents
may also affect how discouraged they become.

The following activities will help children face and overcome their discouragement. With these activities, children can feel comfortable expressing themselves without thinking that adults are prying into their thoughts.

So Long, Worries

Reading *Mom and Dad Break Up* makes it easier for children to open up and express why they are discouraged. Discuss how the little boy in the story feels. Encourage the children to share what they are worried about. Help them express what is the worst possible thing that could happen because of the divorce. Discuss with them what they could do about it. Discuss how they might accept what is happening to their family. Suggest that children write or draw what they fear. Then have them fold their papers and place them in a "worry box." When children find something new to worry about, they can write or draw another picture, fold it and put it in the worry box. Suggest that once children write down their worry and put it in the box, they can stop worrying.

Face Plates

An effective way to help children understand the mixed feelings that accompany divorce is to help them identify how they feel. Suggest that they create face plates to show their feelings. Encourage children to draw various expressions (angry, sad, lonely, hopeless, guilty, scared) on paper plates. Make a hole through all the plates and attach string or yarn to the plate collection. Children can flip the plates to show how they feel. Then discuss the circumstances that brought on each feeling.

Mood Music

Music can help express a child's mood and provide an outlet for emotions. Have children self-select music that expresses their feelings. For discouraged children, try playing loud, fast, or upbeat music. Encourage them to move and dance. For active or angry children, play music that is quiet, slow, and relaxing. Encourage the children to lie down and listen to the music.

Sweet Sharing

Direct the children to close their eyes and pick candy-coated chocolate candies out of a bowl. Tell them they must have a candy-coated chocolate candy in their hand before they can talk. When they pick a red-coated chocolate candy, they share a troubling experience. With a green-coated chocolate candy, they share a good experience. A yellow-coated chocolate candy means they share a wish.

Over and Under

Create an obstacle course using objects in your room such as chairs and tables. Have children hop in a circle, jump backwards or go under the tables. While going through the obstacle course, discuss with children how life isn't always easy, just as the obstacle course isn't easy. Discuss ways of behaving when they're faced with obstacles or problems in their families. Give children the opportunity to discuss problems and to talk about how they solve them.

Memory Book

After a divorce, it may be difficult for children to have contact with a parent. It is comforting for children to have tangible ways to remember the parent. Recommend that they make a scrapbook of pictures and writing—a kind of memory box. Encourage them to think about good times with that parent when the scrapbook is open. But when the scrapbook is put away, it's important to make new memories with new activities and new people.

Feeling Angry

**"Sometimes I felt mad.
I yell at my friends to go away
and pound my pillow."**

These words from the picturebook *Mom and Dad Break Up* convey the angry feelings children have when their parents divorce.

Parental conflict causes problems for children, says Purdue University psychologist Kathryn Black. It doesn't matter whether parents are married or divorced; if parents are fighting, children don't do well.

Children tend to mirror the actions of parents. If parents are angry with each other, it is common for children to respond to their friends and siblings the same way. Unknowingly, children may create a conflict situation so their parents will focus on them instead of focusing on each other. Many children need to work through their feelings of anger caused by divorce. The following activities will give children safe ways to vent their angry feelings without hurting others or themselves.

The "Feel-Angry" Envelope

To help children vent angry feelings, suggest that they cut ten squares of paper. Have them write or dictate on the squares five things about which they're angry with their Mom and five things about which they're angry with their Dad. Have them put the paper squares in "Mom" and "Dad" envelopes. Give children an opportunity to talk about one piece of paper at a time. Listen for insights into their anger without trying to take it away or tell them how to feel. Suggest that they throw away each paper when they feel better or when they forgive the parent. When children become angry about something new, remind them to write it on a piece of paper and try to work through the feeling in the same way.

The "Feel Good" Envelope

To help diffuse some of the anger, suggest that children use ten squares of paper to note five good things about Mom and five good things about Dad. Have them put the papers in "Mom" and "Dad" envelopes. When children feel particularly grumpy, suggest that they read a good thought from these envelopes instead of hanging on to an angry thought.

Why Me?

Sometimes it can be helpful for children to write to their parents about their angry feelings. Often children don't feel listened to, or are too uncomfortable to tell parents what they feel in their hearts. If children are too young to write, urge them to draw a picture. A picture often has more impact than words. Give children the opportunity to mail their messages or pictures, give them to parents, or put them away in a drawer for safe-keeping.

Running Angry

Help children understand that, although it's important to talk about things that bother them, physical activity such as running is a good way to temporarily dispel angry feelings. Suggest that they find a safe place to run with an adult. The local park, stadium, beach, trail, or route to a friend's house can be good places to run.

Pounding Angry

It is not uncommon for children to hit when they are angry. Remind children that even though it's okay to feel angry, it is never okay to hit another person or pet when they are feeling this way. Encourage children to choose something appropriate to hit. A small pillow or bag stuffed with newspaper are good alternatives.

Argue Fairly

Learning to vent anger without harming others or themselves is important. Make a poster to remind children about the rules for "fighting fair":

- Choose *one* thing to argue about.

- Argue about that one thing.

- Talk, don't yell.

- Talk, don't hit or kick.

- Say "I'm sorry" if you know you're wrong.

- Listen to the other person.

- Don't name-call or say hurtful things.

Feeling Sad

"Sometimes I feel sad.
My friend, Anthony, wants me
to go ice skating.
But all I want to do is cry."

These words from the picturebook *Mom and Dad Break Up* convey sad feelings children have when their parents divorce.

Children experience a range of emotions after a divorce, but some children are consumed by sadness for themselves and for their parents.

Young children can sense whether their parents are optimists or pessimists. For children who identify with the pessimistic parent, sadness may become a routine feeling. Children can be sad because their parents are sad, because they don't live with both parents, or because they feel guilty if they stop feeling sad. Explain to children that their sadness won't fix a family. Emphasize that their responses are normal; it's okay to feel sad and, in time, they will feel happy again. Allowing children to express their grief through crying helps them move through the adjustment period.

Activities can help children acknowledge their sadness and understand their feelings.

Rain on My Parade

On a warm day, have children put on their bathing suits or shorts. Give them a garden hose. Suggest they squirt it over their heads straight up in the air. As the water sprinkles down on them like rain, suggest they verbalize the many ways that the divorce *rained on their parade*. Then suggest that their sad feelings and disappointments may be washed away with the water as it seeps into the ground.

Best Memories

Gathering and sorting pictures helps children focus on the fun they had with their families. As they sort their pictures, encourage them to talk about the times they remember. After the sorting process is over, suggest that the children put their favorite pictures into an album that will be a reminder of the good times.

Sharing Time

It is possible for children to get stuck in a rut of sad feelings. It can be helpful to have them list three things they like to do with Mom, Dad, a brother, a sister, another relative, or a friend. Encourage children to choose activities that are inexpensive and easy. When children seem particularly sad, encourage them to choose a person and activity. Have them invite the chosen person by phone, note, or picture to share the "good time." Children can mail or give their invitations to their special friends.

Animal Family

When children are able to express their sadness, they can move on more freely. Let them choose a different stuffed animal to stand for each family member. Suggest they let these stuffed animals "talk" to one another. Listen for insights into children's feelings of sadness. Explain that sadness is a natural feeling and that, in time, much of the sadness will go away.

Chalk It Up

It is often easier for children to express themselves through art. Give them outdoor chalk to use on a concrete playground or sidewalk. Suggest that they draw a picture of their family. Talk with them about what is going on with their family, school, and friends. Listen for insights into how the child is adjusting.

Feeling Lonely

**"Sometimes I feel lonely.
Even when I'm with my friends."**

These words from the picturebook *Mom and Dad Break Up* convey the feelings children have when they experience the loneliness that can follow the divorce of their parents.

Feelings of emptiness and loneliness may swallow up some children shortly after the divorce, especially if there is a custody fight. Children may think that neither parent wants them. The feeling of abandonment can also creep in as children's parents begin to date. Children may feel replaced by the new person in a parent's life. Not knowing how to adjust, some children withdraw into their own worlds.

Sometimes children's lonely feelings and withdrawal are interpreted as anger or sadness.

Creating a new, safe place for children where they don't feel alone helps them adjust to divorce. The following activities may help children understand that they are not alone.

Camp City

One way to help children who are feeling lonely and don't want to play with others is to encourage them to reach out. Suggest that they plan a campout in their backyard, living room, or bedroom. The campers could be brothers, sisters, cousins, or close friends. Suggest that they have a planning meeting to choose a date, to decide on food, sleeping quarters, and games. Often, giving children a project that requires them to think about something else lifts them over the loneliness hump.

Tape It

Another way to help children overcome feelings of loneliness is to encourage them to tape-record each parent singing, telling a story, or reading a book with the child. Suggest that the child listen to the tape when signs of loneliness appear.

Mail It

Consistently sharing events with each parent can help children maintain a secure base. At about the same time each day, direct the children to talk into the tape recorder about how they spent their day. The more comfortable children become with the tape recorder, the more verbal they become. When the tape is complete, mail it to the non-custodial parent. Suggest that children ask their parents to record a tape and mail it back.

Mom Jeff. . . Dad Jeff. . .

Suggest that children name their stuffed animals after the person who gave it to them. Recommend that the animal's last name be the child's first name. For example, If Mom is not around and the child has something to say to Mom, the child could have a conversation and a hug from *Mom Jeff.*

Nature Connection

When children act irritable, stressed, or withdrawn, a walk outside can help them feel more peaceful and safe. Connecting with the great outdoors is an inborn need, according to biologist Edward O. Wilson of Harvard University in Cambridge, Massachusetts. If possible, accompany the children to a nearby park or other recreation area so that they can experience nature.

Kids Care

Children can feel lonely when their families are disrupted. Nevertheless, they can also care about the world around them. Children care about animals that are lost and don't have homes. They care about keeping their city or town free from litter. They care about homeless people. They care about doing well in school. If possible, involve children in a project in which they show interest. Maybe they could take dog food to the pound, pick up litter in a park, or make chili and take it to a homeless shelter.

My Time

Some children may be withdrawn and only seem content if they are working alone on a puzzle, reading, or building with blocks. If children are talking to themselves while playing alone, take the opportunity to observe if they seem lonely or withdrawn. While children need privacy, be aware that some children withdraw too much from family, friends, and activities. Encourage these children to share their puzzle with a friend or sibling, to take turns reading, or to find a friend to help them build with blocks.

Feeling Hopeless

**"Sometimes I dream that Mom and Dad
didn't break up.
I dream that we're all at home the way we're
supposed to be—happy and together.
But then I wake up and realize
it was a dream."**

These words from the picturebook *Mom and Dad Break Up* convey the feelings children have when they experience the hopelessness that often follows the divorce of their parents.

Children of all ages hang on to the belief that their parents will get back together. They tend to forget the unhappiness, the quarreling, even the hostile silences that may have preceded the divorce. Some children simply wish their parents would get back together, while others devise elaborate plans to reunite their parents.

Some children realize that their parents will not remarry, but hang on to the hope that they will see a parent who has moved away or has no time for visits. Help children overcome their feelings of loss by reassuring them that a parent's inability to be with them is not their fault. Reassure the children that they are lovable.

The following activities may help children develop a healthy relationship with each available parent and give up the dream that their parents will get back together. The activities also help children adjust if one parent chooses not to stay involved.

Family Collage
Help children create a collage of photographs showing their family today. Encourage them to draw or find photographs of their family. Encourage children to include photographs of their siblings, uncles, aunts, grandparents, and, of course, parents. Regardless with whom the children live or how frequently they see the non-custodial parent, reassure the children that their mom will always be their mom and their dad will always be their dad. This is what the boy in the picturebook *Mom and Dad Break Up* eventually learned.

My Own Space
Changing children's rooms helps them focus on the present and the future, rather than the past. Moving the bed from one wall to the other, placing a dresser at an angle in the corner, or standing stuffed animals on the floor in the corner instead of on the bed can give a room a whole new look. Encourage children to decorate their rooms with their own art.

My Art Gallery
Give children the opportunity to change the art in their rooms. Discuss changes that occur in life while discussing changes in their art. Discuss with them that even though

they hope their lives won't change, changes occur. Also talk about how their bodies change from year to year. This may help them become more comfortable with the changes taking place in their lives.

Moving On

On a warm day, have children "paint" outdoor furniture or the sidewalk with a bucket of water and a large paintbrush. While the children are water painting, share with them that water is always made of hydrogen and oxygen but has different forms. Ask them to talk about some forms of water that they might know (ice, snow, rain, mist, steam, or vapor). Remind them that water is still water even though it has different forms. Then help them understand that their parents will always be their parents, even though they are divorced. Make them aware that even though they hope their parents will remarry, they probably won't. But their parents will still be their parents, just like water is still water, no matter what its form.

Party Planning

Whether it's a holiday or a regular weekend, suggest that children (with parental consent) invite other single-parent families to their home for a get-together. Assist children in choosing the day, date, time, making the invitations, thinking up the menu, and planning games. Afterward, discuss with them how the party went, reminding them that everyone there was from a single-parent family.

Tomorrow

After a parental breakup, children frequently choose holidays to plan ways to get mom and dad back together. Help children focus their energies in different directions. To help them prepare for holiday fun with family members, suggest that they make gifts, draw pictures, or write stories for parents as well as other family members.

Feeling Guilty

**"Even though I know it wasn't my fault that
Mom and Dad broke up,
sometimes I feel like it was."**

These words from the picturebook *Mom and Dad Break Up* convey the feelings of guilt that children have when their parents divorce.

Children are literal. They believe what others say to them. If they are told that their rooms are always messy or that they are always whining, many children take this to heart and feel that they are bad. Some children feel that being bad means that *they* are responsible for the divorce or separation. This feeling of responsibility often turns into guilt.

Children may try to overcome guilt by being extra good, helping, studying harder, or being extra quiet. They think if they *undo* what they did *wrong*, then their parents will get back together.

Sometimes it is necessary to help children re-focus their energies. The following activities may help children discuss their feelings of guilt and to come to an understanding that they are not responsible for their parents' divorce.

Fill in the Blank
One way to help children overcome their feelings of guilt is to encourage them to share their feelings. Encourage children to complete the following sentences.

If I could, I would _____ , then _____ .

If I had only _____ , then _____ .

I did _____ , then _____ happened.

I didn't _____ , so _____ .

No matter what I said _____ , they _____ .

Even if I _____ .

Because I _____ .

After they complete the sentences, encourage children to talk about their answers. Reassure children that the divorce resulted from a problem between their mom and dad, not because of something the children did or said.

Maybe If
When children exhibit perfectionist behavior, give them an opportunity to discuss why "being good" is important to them. Children may share their guilt over a disagreement with a parent about bedtime or a time when they nagged to watch one more television show. Children may feel that if they had gone to bed or had turned off the television when asked, their parents wouldn't have argued and divorced. Explain to the children that their actions were not the reason for their parents' divorce and that they do not need be perfect to be loved.

Helping Hand

Visiting with and helping people children don't know may take away some of their guilty feelings. The next time you bake brownies or cookies, suggest to children that you drop the goodies off at a daycare center for elders or children, or a Boy's Club or Girl's Club. Because there is no emotional attachment to strangers, children don't expect anything more than a thank-you in return.

Chart It

It is helpful to show children the many ways they are liked and loved. Give them large poster paper to decorate. Suggest that children list or draw actions for which they are liked and/or loved. Actions include: smiling, telling a joke, giving a hug, talking nicely, getting ready for bed, or setting the table. Help children understand that this is not a work chart. Whenever they think of other actions, encourage children to add them to their charts.

A Special Story

Be aware that most children feel loyal to both parents. Whether parents are biological or adoptive, children tend to exhibit traits from both parents. Children frequently experience unsettling feelings when one parent speaks negatively about the other. Children may feel guilty for liking the "bad parent," for favoring a parent, or for being angry at one or both parents. Reassure children that these feelings are normal. Remind them that they may have mixed feelings at one time or another about each parent. Encourage children to write or dictate a story that tells how they are feeling.

Feeling Helpless

**"So I try to put our family back together.
I make surprise parties with
cookies and juice."**

These words from the picturebook *Mom and Dad Break Up* convey the helplessness that children may experience following the divorce of their parents.

Some children are determined to get their parents back together. They think that by doing special favors for their parents they will be able to fix their problems.

Some children feel obligated to take care of their custodial parent. They become helper, spouse, confidant, and caretaker of younger siblings.

Following are some activities to encourage children to help their parents and themselves, without assuming the caretaker role.

Working Together

One way to keep children's helpfulness on track is for parents to work with them on projects such as cooking dinner, working in the garden, and changing beds.

Progressive Dinner

Help children put their party-planning creativity to work outside the family. Get groups of families together and let the children plan a progressive party. If appropriate, plan seasonal outside activities such as swimming, softball, cross-country skiing, or cart rides at the first home. Go to the second home for appetizers. Move on to the third home for a pot-luck dinner, and the fourth house for sweet treats.

Fix It

Find something that needs fixing and ask children to help you fix it. Help children understand that, while they can't fix their parent's marriage, they *can fix* other things. This gives children a feeling of control over their lives and helps them accept the divorce.

Pet Care

Feeding, watering, walking, playing, and loving pets redirects children's helpfulness and nurturing where it is needed and wanted. Pets such as goldfish, gerbils, and turtles are easy pets to care for.

Garden Goodies

Invite children to plan and then plant a vegetable garden in a small area of the yard or an herb garden in a window box. Caring for the garden, watching it grow, and harvesting a crop lets children feel helpful in positive ways. Encourage children to share the produce/herbs with others.

Feeling Sick

**"I even pretend that I'm really, really sick
and need both of them
to make me better."**

These words from the picturebook *Mom and Dad Break
Up* convey the feeling of real or "pretend" sickness that
children can experience following their parents' divorce.

Remember that the stress of divorce often shows up in a
variety of behaviors and physical symptoms. Children may
show signs of sickness when they are emotionally upset.

Using the following activities, encourage children to talk
about the feelings they may have felt since the divorce, such

as anger, fear, sadness, loneliness, and guilt. Notice whether or not their physical symptoms, if any, disappear. If the symptoms do not disappear, encourage the child's parent or caregiver to seek professional medical attention for the child.

"X" Marks the Spot

If a child complains of a stomachache but shows no other symptoms, explore other possible sources of the stomachache. Draw a picture of a person on a large piece of paper. Have the child make an **X** on the parts of the body where the pain or pains are. Encourage the child to tell about each pain, when it started and how it feels. After the child talks about the pains, encourage the child to talk about angry, sad, or lonely feelings. After the discussion, ask for an update about the pains. The pains may have diminished or vanished. Reaching for medicine, instead of looking for root emotional issues, may do a child a disservice. If complaints continue, it is wise to seek professional care.

For the Record

Children may want to share what is happening in their lives, but children share in different ways. For those children who like to write, fold several pieces of paper in half and suggest they write or dictate a picturebook about what is going on in their family. Give them colored pencils, crayons, or markers to draw illustrations. Some children may express angry or sad feelings; others may not. Sharing unpleasant experiences and feelings improves physical and mental health. Burying unpleasant feelings increases the risk of illness.

Love You and Like You

It is common for some children to feel that if their parents don't love each other, they must not love them, either. Not knowing what to do with this worry can actually make children feel ill. Draw a happy face with a giant mouth on a paper plate for each child. Cut out the mouth. Glue a paper lunch bag behind the mouth. Encourage children to write reasons why their parents love them on small pieces of paper. Have the children fold the pieces of paper and put them in the mouth. When the children feel ill or sad, suggest that they reach into the happy face mouth to remember why they are lovable.

Love Me Anyway

Some younger children may regress to thumb-sucking, wetting their pants, or clinginess during a divorce. Eating and sleeping problems are common, too. Some children become aggressive or revert to hitting, biting, or yelling. Focusing on positive behavior helps children return to their old selves more quickly. Distribute colored construction paper to children. Encourage them to draw pictures of positive actions on the paper, such as waving good-bye to a custodial parent without crying. When children repeat positive actions, have them add stars next to their pictures.

Stress Mess

To help children understand that they have some control over their lives, have them write, dictate, or draw examples of the following:

- areas in which where they are likely to have control, such as choosing the clothes they wear, the books they read, or the toys they play with.

- people, other than their parents, who are important to them.

- How their family situation might be better in a year.

Help children understand that controlling stress helps them maintain better health.

Feeling Scared

The cover illustration from the picturebook *Mom and Dad Break Up* conveys the frightened feeling many children experience during their parents' divorce.

Children need the security of knowing that their physical and emotional needs are being met. After a divorce, children perceive that their basic needs will not be met. This can lead to scared feelings: *What about me? Who will take care of me?* Some children may worry excessively about a custodial parent's health. Young children feel that, having already "lost" one parent, they may lose the custodial parent, too.

It is common for children to have feelings of fear and apprehension. With these activities, children may feel more comfortable about one or both of their parents being there to care for them.

Share Your Schedule

Not knowing where a parent is can be scary for children. Even though children may be left with responsible adults, some still fear that their parent won't come back. It's comforting for children to know where their parents are going and approximately when they will return. For a younger child, setting the hands on a play clock is helpful. For an older child, writing a schedule on a chalkboard works well. Telephoning or leaving a message on an answering machine reassures children that their parents are all right.

Notes to You

The briefest note can make the biggest difference in reassuring children that their parents are there for them. Parents can put notes in lunch boxes, pants pockets, or tape them to mirrors. Children can return notes to their parents and put them under coffee cups, in briefcases, or under pillows.

Feeling Better

**"We don't all live together anymore.
But I know my Mom will always be my Mom.
And we'll have hugs.**

These words from the picturebook *Mom and Dad Break Up* convey the feeling of acceptance that children will come to experience after their parents are divorced.

Share with children the idea that there are changes throughout life. Some changes are good: making a new friend, getting a pet, or visiting relatives. Some changes involve disappointments: divorce, illness, or having a friend move away. Understanding what precipitated the disappointing change, working through the accompanying feelings, and accepting the change helps children feel better.

**And my Dad will always be my Dad.
And we'll have hugs."**

Help children understand and accept divorce through the
following activities.

Making New Memories
Start a "Let's Do" book. Suggest that children list activities
they want to do when they are with Mom and activities they
want to do when they are with Dad. Explain that activities
don't have to be expensive to be special. Reading together,
biking, or hiking are some easy and inexpensive activities.
Help children understand that they are building new
memories, so it may be fun to try new activities.

Hugs to You

Hugs feel good. Studies suggest that everyone needs between seven and twelve hugs a day. Encourage children to hug their moms and dads. It's impossible for children to know all that is going on in their parents' lives; it might be easier for a parent to give and receive a hug than to talk. Children love hugs and are comforted by them, too. Suggest that children give hugs to feel better.

Family Night

Instead of watching television, encourage children to plan a family afternoon or evening with a parent. A hike, bike ride, family baseball game, or barbecue followed by a board game brings the family together and helps to build new memories.

Let's Meet

Airing feelings is sometimes easier at a family meeting. The following guidelines should make the meeting run smoothly. Select a soft object and make it clear that only the person holding the object can talk. When someone wants to speak, he or she gestures for the object. Use a timer to limit talking time. Talking time should be the same for adults and children. To make sure everyone shares what is important, direct each person to come with a list of things to talk about.

Flag It

Recommend that children create flags celebrating each of their families. If appropriate, suggest that children include stepparents, half- or step-brothers and sisters, and pets. To do this activity, fold a paper into several squares. Each square represents a family member about whom children can draw or write something. If there are extra squares, save them for new members that come into the family. When children visit their seperate homes, suggest they "fly" their flags.

Afterthoughts

Although children who are experiencing divorce may appear to be fine, divorce is most often traumatic. There are many areas of children's lives that may change, such as:

- Family structure
- Contact with one or both parents
- Time spent with parents
- Time spent with siblings
- Financial stability
- Living situation
- Pets
- School
- Friends
- After-school activities

Since change produces feelings, It is common for some children experiencing divorce to have feelings of:

- shock
- discouragement
- anger
- sadness
- loneliness
- hopelessness
- guilt
- helplessness
- sickness
- fear

Children need to express and respond to their feelings. Give them the opportunity to respond without being judged. Just because children don't openly share their feelings doesn't mean they don't have any. Remember, for every action such as divorce, there is a feeling. And for every feeling there is a response. Talking, writing, dictating, singing, or drawing are examples of constructive responses. Sometimes, gentle prodding encourages children to respond. Some suggested questions for a parent to ask children follow. Let the children choose how they want to respond. Try not to interrupt children while they are talking.

- What has been difficult for you?

- How do you feel about Dad? About Mom?

- What do you think of Dad dating? Mom dating?

- What do you think about the family now?

- How would you describe the family now?

- How do you feel about my working?

- What makes you feel angry?

- What makes you feel sad?

- What is your biggest fear?

- When do you feel lonely?

- What do you dream about?

- What would you like to change?

Additional Resources

Atlas, Stephen L. *The Official Parents Without Partners Sourcebook*. Philadelphia, PA: Running Press, 1984.

This manual offers practical advice and personal experiences from single parents on a range of topics including finances, decision-making, discipline, communication, custody issues, and special needs.

Brazelton, T. Berry, M.D. *Working and Caring*. Reading, MA: Addison-Wesley, 1985.

Here is sensible and comforting advice for the working parent from the well-known pediatrician and child development expert, who balances his empathy for the parent with his concern for the child's well-being.

Einstein, Elizabeth. *The Stepfamily: Living, Loving & Learning*. Boston, MA: Shambhala Publications, 1985.

   This book, written by a woman who is both a stepdaughter and a stepmother, provides information and advice on how to keep blended families together and maximize their potential for happiness and fulfillment; a sensitive exploration of the difficulties faced and ways to overcome them.

Elkind, David, Ph.D. *The Hurried Child: Growing Up Too Fast Too Soon*. Reading, MA: Addison-Wesley, 1981.

   Dr. Elkind discusses how early misinformation can cause permanent damage to a child's self-esteem and subsequent attitude toward learning.

Ephron, Delia. *Funny Sauce, the Ex, the Ex's New Mate, the Mate's Ex, and the Kids*. New York: Viking Press, 1986.

   Hilarious, wise, comic, and insightful, Ms. Ephron shares stories about her husband and two stepchildren.

Hart, Archibald D., Ph.D. *Stress and Your Child*. Dallas, TX: Word, 1992.

   Practical book packed with up-to-date information and down-to-earth guidance (including nine "stress tests" and two worksheets) to understand stress, pinpoint stress points, help handle stress, and more.

Kalter, Neil, Ph.D. *Growing Up with Divorce: Helping Your Child Avoid Immediate and Later Emotional Problems*. New York: Free Press/Macmillan, 1989.

   Presents a clear, compassionate, developmental approach to protecting children from the emotional fallout of divorce. The author provides invaluable guidance that helps parents and children cope with the problems specific to their situation.

Keshet, Jamie K. *Love and Power in the Stepfamily*. New York: McGraw-Hill, 1986.

Advice and strategies offered by a family therapist who specializes in working with blended families.

Lansky, Vicki. *Vicki Lansky's Divorce Book for Parents: Helping Your Children Cope with Divorce and Its Aftermath*. New York: American Library, 1989.

This practical and warmly supportive manual goes step-by-step through all the stages of separation and divorce. Lansky gives advice that is age-specific for children and explains what kind of reactions to expect, how to respond, and when to seek professional advice.

Neifert, Marianne, M.D. *Dr. Mom's Parenting Guide*. New York: Dutton, 1991.

Filled with practical wisdom and a positive, realistic philosophy of parenting drawn from her experience as both a pediatrician and mother of five. The book covers children from the first exciting days of life to the stormy seas of adolescence.

Rosin, Mark Bruce. *Stepfathering: Stepfathers' Advice on Creating a New Family*. New York: Simon & Schuster, 1987.

Providing advice and encouragement for men by men, this book presents the headaches, heartaches, and joys of raising stepchildren, written from personal experience and in-depth interviews with more than fifty stepfathers.

Schaefer, Charles E., Ph.D. *How to Talk to Children About Really Important Things*. New York: Harper and Row, 1984.

Provides guidelines, strategies, and tips on how to talk with children and how to be an *approachable* parent. Schaefer stresses the importance of listening to and acknowledging the child's viewpoint.

Siegel-Gorelick, Bryna, Ph.D. *The Working Parents' Guide to Child Care.* Boston: Little, Brown & Co., 1983.

Solid information on the various options for child care and guidance on deciding which choice is best for your child. Reflects practical advice on issues such as interviewing, contracts, child development, and attachment concerns.

Smith, Dian G. *Raising Kids in a Changing World.* New York: Prentice Hall Press, 1991.

Constructive information and guidelines for what children need to learn about themselves and the world around them to realize their potential.

Thomas Nelson Publishers. *The Family Matters Handbook.* Nashville: Thomas Nelson Publishers, 1994.

Thirty-one doctors and counselors came together to create this comprehensive volume as a how-to guide for building a secure, nurturing family atmosphere.

Weiss, Robert S., Ph.D. *Going It Alone: The Family Life and Social Situation of the Single Parent.* New York: Basic Books, 1981.

Sociologist Weiss discusses the life of the single parent. In their own words, single parents relate the everyday problems of raising children, coping mechanisms, and how they feel.

Books for Children

Good children's books are excellent for stimulating conversation about feelings and emotions. Children, regardless of age, will usually respond by listening, thinking, imagining, and then expressing their thoughts. Reading a book about a similar experience that a child is facing can help children work through and perhaps resolve their feelings. Reading helps children realize that they are not alone.

The following is an annotated bibliography of some fiction and non-fiction literature dealing with emotions that are appropriate for preschool to third-grade children. Choose the books that best suit the needs of the children in your care.

Brown, Laurene Krasny, and Marc Brown. *Dinosaurs Divorce*. Boston: Little, Brown & Co., 1986.

Simple text and humorous illustrations of dinosaur families make this a timely and reassuring resource for young children and their parents with positive suggestions for handling the new and difficult situations and feelings that divorce can bring.

Cleary, Beverly. *Dear Mr. Henshaw*. Illustrated by Paul O. Zelinsky. New York: William Morrow, 1983.

This Newbery Award winner is funny, sad, and very real. A lonely fourth grader corresponds with his favorite author revealing how much he wishes his divorced parents would remarry, how much he misses his dad, and how he negotiates the trials of school.

Clifton, Lucille. *Everett Anderson's 1-2-3*. Illustrated by Ann Grifalconi. New York: Holt, Rinehart, and Winston, 1977.

When his mother starts seeing Mr. Perry, Everett starts thinking about numbers: One is lonely, two is just right, and three is too crowded. Mama's new happiness helps Everett change his mind.

Goff, Beth. *Where is Daddy?* Illustrated by Susan Perl. Boston: Beacon Press, 1985.

A little girl suffers from many fears when her parents divorce. Her mother and grandmother come to realize that she needs extra assurance and an explanation of the events taking place.

Grollman, Earl A. *Talking About Divorce*. Illustrated by Allision Cann. Boston: Beacon Press, 1975.

Dialogue between parent and child helps small children of divorcing parents understand and accept that their parents are no longer married. Includes a parent guide.

Hazen, Barbara Shook. *Two Homes to Live In*. Illustrated by Peggy Luks. New York: Human Sciences Press, 1978.

A little girl explains how she came to terms with her parents divorce.

Jukes, Mavis. *Like Jake and Me*. Illustrated by Lloyd Bloom. New York: Alfred A. Knopf, 1984.

Jake and his new stepson, Alex, realize that they have a lot in common in a warm, humorous story of a loving family.

Support Groups

American Association for Marriage and Family

1717 K Street, Northwest, Suite 407
Washington, DC 20006
202/429-1825

Directory of clinical members and approved supervisors in marriage and family therapy.

Child Care Action Campaign (CCAC)

330 Seventh Avenue, 18th floor
New York, New York 10001
212/239-0138

The goal of this organization is to establish a national system of quality, affordable child care. It publishes information guides summarizing important family issues.

National Self-Help Clearinghouse

33 West 42nd Street
New York, New York 10036

For information of support groups, send a letter describing your circumstances with a self-addressed stamped envelope.

Parents Without Partners, Inc.

8807 Colesville Road
Silver Spring, Maryland 20910
800/638-8078

This organization offers services to single parents and their children to aid in crisis intervention and education.

Single Mothers by Choice

P.O. Box 1642, Gracie Square Station
New York, New York 10028
212/988-0993

For women who have chosen or are considering single motherhood, information, and moral support are available.

Stepfamily Foundation, Inc.

333 West End Avenue
New York, New York 10023
212/877-3244

Provides information, conducts seminars, and creates awareness of problems in step-relationships.

Kids Have Feelings, Too series

written by Joan Singleton Prestine
illustrated by Virginia Kylberg

The **Kids Have Feelings, Too** series was created to help parents, teachers, and caregivers deal constructively with the feelings children have as a result of traumatic events in their lives such as death and divorce; or of simply growing up, such as learning to share. Each **Kids Have Feelings, Too** package includes a picturebook to share with children, and a resource guide full of activities and practical suggestions for helping children respond positively to their feelings and emotions.

In the *Someone Special Died* picturebook, a young girl learns how to deal with the death of a loved one. Her feelings range from denial to anger to bargaining to sadness before she makes a scrapbook and accepts the death. She realizes that her loved one won't come back, but that she'll always have her happy memories. 1994 Parents' Choice Parenting Shelf Award.

The accompanying resource guide, *Helping Children Cope with Death*, is designed to help adults assist children through the uncomfortable feelings children can have after the death of someone a child loves. Without telling children how to feel or respond, 61 activities provide the information necessary for adults to feel confident helping children help themselves through the grieving process. 1994 Parents' Choice Parenting Shelf Award.

In the *Sometimes I Feel Awful* picturebook, a little girl begins her day feeling happy. Through a series of actions, she experiences a variety of feelings and emotions and responds to these emotions in many ways.

The accompanying resource guide, *Helping Children Understand Their Feelings*, provides practical suggestions and activities for communicating with children, recognizing their emotions, and helping children learn to respond in constructive, positive ways to the 14 emotions presented in the picturebook *Sometimes I Feel Awful*.

In the *It's Hard to Share My Teacher* picturebook, Josh discovers it's easier to share things, than it is to share his teacher. Josh finally realizes he has to share everything in school, even his teacher.

Helping Children Share Their Teacher provides 77 practical activities for adults to help children gradually learn how to share—share toys, school supplies, feelings and, eventually, their teacher.

Index